The little book of Negotiat

Dedication

I would like to dedicate this book to my two sons (Adam and Jack Johnson) who have been with me every step of the way throughout my career and who are my absolute lifeblood. My Mother who has supported me with dog sitting, house cleaning and just by being there. To the many mentors that I have depended on throughout my career, and to all of my clients who have stood by my side through thick and thin and have developed their people and raised their organisation's bar on commercial negotiation capability through choosing SLP Consulting & Training Ltd as their preferred partner over other Global Negotiation Consultancy giants out there. I cherish these relationships and from the bottom of my heart THANK YOU. I really couldn't have written this book without every single one of you.

The little book of Negotiation Brilliance

Client Testimonial

Antonio Barbetta – Global Procurement Director

"*...Sue Preston, has been a passionate, focussed teacher, consultant, coach and leader in the science and art of professional negotiations.*
Having worked with her over the years, I could never help myself feeling, and leaving, inspired and richer in knowledge from her many Negotiations sessions. This great book is both a testament and natural consequence of all of Sue's hard work and thought leadership which she has passed to so many over the years. Above all it is a testament to the top professional, consultant and subject leader she is. I for one am very proud of all her accomplishments, and this book is a Negotiation reference that I intend to keep close to me."

The little book of Negotiation Brilliance

Introduction and Why read?

Let's start with what's in it for you and why you should read this book. It is an easy read that gives you the toolkit required for successful negotiation outcomes. The toolkit is packed with proven techniques and strategies which work in today's tough business world globally. It is practical and instantly applicable in any market and focuses on both sides of the buyer/seller interface.

This book is a MUST read whether you are negotiating in a tactical/competitive marketplace or a complex one that requires strategic collaboration.   Whatever market you are operating in you need to remember that Negotiation is a people-based activity and the degree to which you build, or engineer rapport is critical to the success of the outcome e.g. If the other party has power in a complex negotiation and you have little to no power, then they are more likely to stick to their own objectives if they don't like you. (Rhetorical question time…. Do you like everyone you negotiate with?)   Sometimes all we have in our favour is the power of persuasion, personal impact and digging deep to utilise every last spec of emotional intelligence we can muster. If you build a deep level of rapport and they like you, they are more likely to give you some of what they have to give.   E.g. your teenagers have more chance of getting extra money from you if they remain likeable. Any teenage 'attitude' and parents will stick to their guns and the result of possible grounding becomes all too real.

The little book of Negotiation Brilliance

From a buyer perspective what about when you are in a position where you need to secure supply as not having that product or service is high risk to the future of your organisation?

From a seller perspective what about when you want to secure that account that would be core to your organisation, is highly attractive in terms of its brand and is likely to spend a lot of money with you. When relationship is key the deeper the level of rapport the more likely you are to secure supply or win that 'core' account.

You need to consider the many layers of culture within Negotiation and what might be different when negotiating with suppliers or buyers that are based in other countries and how that might affect successful outcomes. Also, considerations on low cost country sourcing for buyers. Is cheap always best?

Remember that culture has many complex layers and is not one dimensional. Culture is National, Organisational, Departmental, Individual and Environmental. Being culture savvy when negotiating is key to the outcome of your interactions both with internal stakeholders and external suppliers or customers. For more information on culture visit www.hofstede-insights.com. Gert Hofstede has a phenomenal website which I constantly use when negotiating on behalf of clients based overseas.

The little book of Negotiation Brilliance

This little book of Negotiation Brilliance will become your 'Go To' negotiation mentor and coach no matter what market, culture or which side of the buyer/seller interface you operate. This book is practical, and the toolkit is immediately applicable to real life. Each chapter includes reflection areas to ensure your investment in reading each section results in value for you and your organisation in every negotiation.

I will share some of my commercial negotiation experiences with you from the UK/Europe to USA, Russia, Bangkok, Istanbul/Turkey, Australia and other countries that I have negotiated in.

The little book of Negotiation Brilliance

The Little Book of Negotiation Brilliance?

'REAL' Negotiation Challenges	Frequently Asked Questions that will be answered within this book of Negotiation Brilliance
BUT....... Am I 'really' Negotiating?	What do we mean by negotiation and who will benefit from the Negotiation Brilliance Toolkit?
Why tight rope walkers are the best Negotiators	The tight Rope Walk - Best approach to all negotiations whether you are buying a car or involved in multimillion-dollar negotiations
The Negotiation Mastery Ladder -*Every stage to successful outcomes*	Structure, Preparation & Planning, questioning techniques and Proposing your deal
Gaining movement; Zero power and monopoly situations	Influencing and Persuading others when you have little to no power
Rolling the dice	Tactics we deploy and techniques for recognising and countering tactics used by the other party
The Emotionally Intelligent Negotiator	Magic wands and staying 100% present
Takeaways and Appendices	Documents for downloading. To use in your 'REAL' negotiations

The little book of Negotiation Brilliance

IN SUMMARY...THE AIM IS FOR YOU TO HAVE A PRACTICAL TOOLKIT RATHER THAN A TEXTBOOK THAT STAYS ON THE SHELF OR IN YOUR DOWNLOAD FILE AND NEVER SEES THE LIGHT OF DAY.

Be prepared to complete exercises as you progress through the book and capture information in the thought boxes keeping an imminent (tough) negotiation in mind. By the end of this book you will be better prepared than ever before. The toolkit in the book is based on approaches and strategies I have used when negotiating on behalf of clients in most parts of the world.

The little book of Negotiation Brilliance

'REAL' NEGOTIATION CHALLENGES

On my travels around the world I am frequently asked similar questions which I will share with you now. Of course the answer to most of them is ... "it depends" on several things e.g. who you are negotiating with, the importance of the outcome over the relationship, the relationship you have/need with the other party, the personal dynamics and personalities involved, the market you are operating in, supply and demand issues, culture, the power balance and several other areas, which is why personal coaching and guidance is the best way to get clear answers to specific complex questions.

Here's an example of some of the more generic questions I am asked, the answers to which you will find within this book. These questions will be printed again at the end of the book. Answer them now with your current knowledge and answer them again at the end of the book. Then compare any differences and create an action plan of changes you need to make to your negotiation approach.

- When's the right time to put your stake in the ground?
- How can I negotiate with a monopoly supplier?
- How do you get the other party to say 'YES'?
- How do you regain control?
- What should you do when you hit stalemate?

The little book of Negotiation Brilliance

- How do you know the other party's 'true' range of objectives?
- What are the key signals of movement?
- Is there ever a time where you just put all your cards on the table, refuse to play the game and just tell the other party what you need?
- Where is the best location for a Negotiation? Home or Away?
- What is the optimum number for a successful negotiation team?
- What are the responsibilities and key roles in team negotiations?
- Why are some people innately good negotiators?
- How do I secure a better deal when I need the product/service delivered quickly?
- How does supply and demand affect the outcome of Negotiation?
- What is a good amount of time to set aside for Preparation and Planning?
- What is the difference between internal and external negotiations?
- How does culture affect negotiations?
- How do you deal with difficult people during a negotiation?

The little book of Negotiation Brilliance

BUT….AM I REALLY NEGOTIATING?
What do we mean by Negotiation and who will benefit from the toolkit?

STARTER CHALLENGE
Before reading further write in the box below your definition of Negotiation in just one word. (That word cannot be Negotiation ☺)

I'm sure you have a variety of words such as bargain, trade, objectives, win-win, outcome, compromise, agreement etc. The one word that really sums up Negotiation is MOVEMENT. Have you ever been in a situation where you are presenting your logic and compelling argument, but the other party just doesn't get it? This usually results in nothing more than a circular argument. You don't see his/her logic and they don't see yours. This is detrimental to any negotiation so a reminder "When you have stopped moving you have stopped negotiating" you are simply in a circular argument of he said, she said. Specifically, in the trading phase we need to remember the art of Negotiation is moving from our 'Utopia' position to a point where agreement may be reached. ***STOP PRESS*** – Am I arguing or Am I negotiating?

The little book of Negotiation Brilliance

MOVEMENT – of course isn't a full definition of Negotiation Brilliance. The art requires a structure, people interaction, emotional intelligence, strategies, tactics, preparation. The list goes on.

Our mindset is key when entering into a negotiation, so we need to be careful what we wish for. For example, if you enter into a negotiation expecting to deal with conflict guess what you'll get…yup! conflict. Self-fulfilling prophecy – "What you think will happen probably will". When you peel back to the origin of the word Negotiation its journey started in the Latin language where the word 'negotiatus' came from 'negotiari'. Negotiari's literal translation is; "to carry on business". So, what does all this mean for us? If we enter a negotiation with a mindset 'To do business' that's exactly what will happen we will participate in the act of 'doing business'. If we enter into a negotiation with the mindset of 'managing conflict' that's exactly what we will get…conflict. Start as you mean to go on and read further to uncover the Negotiation Brilliance Toolkit which will help you to be consistently successful when entering into negotiations with the 'To do business' mantra.

The little book of Negotiation Brilliance

In summary – Whatever level of Negotiator you are you need to remember that negotiation is a people-based activity that requires exquisite communication skill and a robust strategy to ensure you strive to hit a favourable outcome.

In the box below write yourself a clear definition of Negotiation taking into account everything discussed in this chapter.

The little book of Negotiation Brilliance

WHY TIGHT ROPE WALKERS ARE THE BEST NEGOTIATORS
In this next chapter we explore the best approach to all negotiations from buying a car to closing a multimillion-dollar deal

No-one ever said the job of a skilled negotiator was an easy one. You have to ensure your balancing act is 'on point' to ensure you get the best out of the other party. Some people are innately pleasant and congenial in their approach to others and its true to say some people are innately task driven and focussed only on the outcome of the deal. Whichever side of the tight rope you fall you will miss out on securing even better outcomes unless you achieve a balance between being likeable and focussed. If you were to model negotiation excellence, you have to start with the behaviours of successful negotiators. Complete the box below; have someone in mind that you aspire to in terms of their negotiation ability and list the behaviours, tools and characteristics they deploy to achieve success.

The little book of Negotiation Brilliance

There are many traits that successful negotiators have such as:

Emotional intelligence, Persistence, Good communication skills, Articulate, Great listeners, well prepared, Adaptable, Strategic Thinker, Creative, Knowledgeable, Assertive, Confident, Intuitive, Journalistic, Responsive, Likeable, Focussed, Skilful

Food for thought before we move on; Is it easier for me to give up something I have (and you want) if I like you or dislike you? ...
If I like you of course.   If I have power in a Negotiation and we have zero rapport, then why would I give you something I have?   Think of teenagers when they need £10 to go into town for a coffee with their mates.   If they ask politely and with respect, they are more likely to get something from us.   If they are belligerent and disrespectful, they are unlikely to get anything.   Same in the commercial world.

It is true to say that the balance of being likeable and focussed/persistent in your negotiations is not always 50/50 to each side.   If the other party has all the power in a negotiation, the only thing you have in your armoury to gain movement is your ability to build rapport. So, I would suggest although we don't want to appear 'weak' we would allocate a balance of 80% to likeability and 20% to

The little book of Negotiation Brilliance

focus/persistence. If, however, you have the power in a competitive market then the 80/20 balance can be reversed to 80% focussed and persistent and 20% likeability. The moral of the story is the balance on the tight rope is dependent on which markets you are operating in. Suffice to say that balance is always made up of likeability and focus/persistence.

One example of when I have experienced negotiating with a buying team who ceremoniously fell off the tight rope. "I was negotiating with a Category Manager who was doing a great job. I liked the guy, we had a good level of rapport and he was assertive and focussed on his objectives as well as having consideration for mine, a pretty balanced walk on the tight rope.   As a lot of facts and figures started to fly around, I summarised and called a break-off to slow the pace down and maintain control. When we re-entered the room the Category Manager was accompanied by his boss who had an aggressive and competitive approach. The boss stated (without any consideration for a tight rope balance) "I need to tell you that we will not pay your quoted prices, you have to reduce them by at least 15% otherwise we have no deal". His boss undid all the great work of the Category Manager and the frustration was evident from his facial expression. I summarised again including their need for a more collaborative approach and stated in a warm, assertive and persistent manner how his new demand wouldn't be possible, but I would leave them to discuss the next steps

The little book of Negotiation Brilliance

and wished them well.   This is an example of why the tight rope walk is so important.   Ensure the other party finds you likeable and trustworthy without compromising your assertion and focus on your objectives.   I had the power to walk because had I remained in the room the deal he demanded would not have been commercially viable for me or my team.

So, the best approach to all negotiations whether you are buying a car or closing a multimillion-dollar deal is finding the correct balance to navigate the tight rope walk.   Too much on the side of your own objectives and you break rapport and damage the relationship.   Too much focus on being lovely, gorgeous and liked you will lose out on the final outcome.

The little book of Negotiation Brilliance

BARRIERS TO SECURING A GREAT DEAL

Reflect on past Negotiations you have been involved in. What would you have done differently? What went wrong? Why did you hit stalemate? Why did you get into circular arguments? List all your reflections in the box below.

Keep this list to hand and once you reach the end of the book, revisit and make notes of how you can prevent these things happening next time? What tools can you take from this book to help in your next Negotiation? If you are left with blanks for some of your dilemmas email me Sue@Sueprestontraining.com and I will organise a virtual call with you and provide guidance and coaching.

The little book of Negotiation Brilliance

There are many barriers to negotiating and some can easily be corrected. E.g. How do you feel if the other party addresses you as Honey, Love, Mate, Buddy? For some of us those labels work fine but for others they create defensive reactions. Take your lead from the other party, if they address you Mr, Mrs, Miss then reciprocate and address them similarly until you have built a deep enough level of rapport to use first names. This, I'm afraid, is less about you and more about the other party. Remember, people like people like themselves, take your lead from them in terms of introductions. This is about gaining trust and building rapport to drive win-win in a collaborative environment or secure a good deal in a competitive one.

Care re *'telling'* people they have to move and reduce their prices, improve delivery or demand more for less; this again will cause defensive reactions. You are looking for the other party to respond in a way that builds relationships (even transactional) and secures a good deal. The only option you have is to *'persuade and influence'* in a way that is acceptable to both parties.

Other barriers on your list probably include not listening, interrupting, aggression, indecisive, untrustworthy, belligerence and sometimes being over familiar. By the end of this book you will have an awareness of when you may be using these barriers unintentionally, and a toolkit to manage your response when barriers are used by you or the other party.

The little book of Negotiation Brilliance

THE MASTERY LADDER TO SUCCESSFUL OUTCOMES
Every stage from preparation to proposing to success

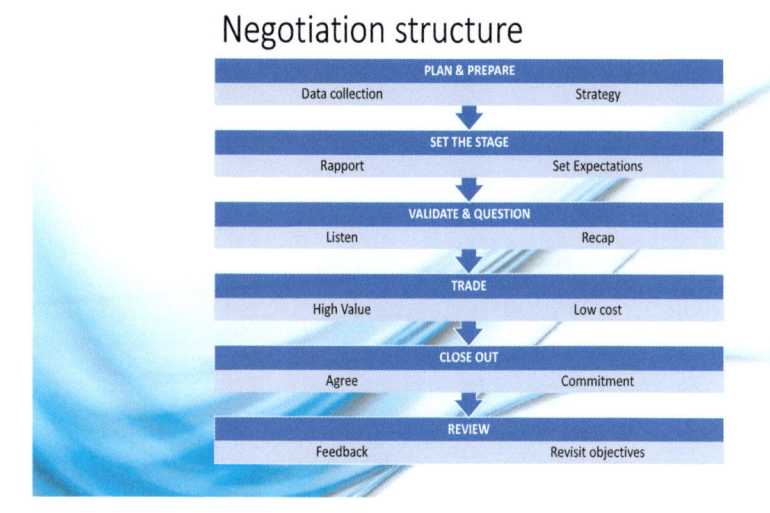

Negotiation structure

PLAN & PREPARE	
Data collection	Strategy

SET THE STAGE	
Rapport	Set Expectations

VALIDATE & QUESTION	
Listen	Recap

TRADE	
High Value	Low cost

CLOSE OUT	
Agree	Commitment

REVIEW	
Feedback	Revisit objectives

STAGE 1 PLAN AND PREPARE

The old adage "What you do or don't do in preparation and planning will reflect in the outcome of any deal" is absolutely true. You are there to secure a great deal and not there on a wing and a prayer to see what you come out with. There is no-one in this world that can give you more hours in the day, time is a commodity we all have the same amount of. It is true however, that if you don't have time to plan well it will cost you in the final outcome. We need to be smarter in our preparedness for great negotiation outcomes which means; having planning and

The little book of Negotiation Brilliance

preparation templates for different types of negotiation. E.g. I have 3 templates (which you can obtain by contacting me at Sue@sueprestontraining.com).

Template 1 is my quick and dirty method of preparing for quick wins that take less time. E.g. A few years ago, I rented a flat. A potential rental came on the market and I had to drop everything and shoot over to Eastbourne within a moment's notice as these apartments get snatched up pretty quickly. I arrived 10 minutes before the letting agent and sat in my car. On the back of an old envelope I planned as quickly but efficiently as possible for the negotiation as the advertised monthly rent was way above my budget. I used my quick and dirty method of preparation as I had limited time. Once the letting agent arrived, I was ready to rock and roll and yes, I secured a reduction off the monthly rent and a moving in date that suited me perfectly. I was in the flat within 2 weeks and lived there for over 2 years.

Template 2 is a more structured process and used to prepare and plan for negotiations that are of higher value. This template is included in the book (appendix 1). You will find 1,000's of these completed templates on my laptop and in my office. I use Template 2 more regularly in commercial settings as it provides a more thorough approach to being well prepared. If you are negotiating in a more tactical or competitive environment with an outcome that has high importance for your organisation, see (appendix 1).

The little book of Negotiation Brilliance

Template 3 is a detailed, time consuming template for complex negotiations. E.g. capex machinery, large construction projects, large IT infrastructure projects. Those negotiations that are high risk to your organisation in respect of not securing a deal.   Are your production lines at risk of stopping? Is the specification of what you are buying extremely high? Are you in a monopoly situation where there is only 1 supplier globally that could deliver? Are you selling to a potential new client which would secure entry into a new market for your organisation? Is the potential value of this sale extremely high and a real coup for your organisation? Would securing this sale put you ahead in terms of market share in your industry? Is this a big-ticket item with huge impact? If the answer to any of the pre mentioned questions is yes, then you have no choice but to complete due diligence and ensure you are prepared and planned for all eventualities.   In these circumstances invest the time, pull together cross functional teams and run internal workshops to ensure your planning and preparation is robust.   The template details your strategy and the strategy of the other party (of course it relies on assumptions at the preparation stage which you would need to validate during the process of negotiation).
This detailed template can be obtained by contacting Sue@sueprestontraining.com

The little book of Negotiation Brilliance

If preparing and planning in time starved environments read my article for practical tips (appendix 2).

PREPARATION AND PLANNING 101 – The 'musts' when negotiating in any scenario.
Analyse the market you are operating in and select the correct approach for that market dynamic.   In competitive/tactical negotiations your objective is to 'highlight' difference and in collaborative/strategic negotiations your objective is to 'minimise' difference.

List all of your key variables for the negotiation.   What are you prepared to move on? what will the other party want you to move on? what variables are critical to this Negotiation? e.g. Price, Quality, Quantity, Delivery, Timescales etc.   for each variable you need to set a target of what *utopia* looks like.   "If I were to go back to the business and celebrate an achievement what would that look like? What would give me instant promotion?".   Next you need a more *likely* position.   After researching the market, competitors, comparative offers, the other party where are you most likely to agree.   And then you need a position that, if pushed, you will decline, walk away from and refuse to Negotiate further, this is your **No-Go** target. If we reflect on one of the first things mentioned in this book in terms of the one word to define Negotiation being 'MOVEMENT' the clue is in the title.   We need to move in order to be negotiating.   No Movement = An argument. When you hit a circular argument and there is zero

The little book of Negotiation Brilliance

movement you will not progress towards your desired outcome. Remember; your logic is your perception of truth and the other party will have their own perception. In any argument there is always your truth, the other party's truth and the actual truth. If the other party doesn't see your logic don't go in for the fight to win or enthusiastically try to convince them as it could result in losing all rapport and could even be detrimental to the outcome of your deal. Be creative and find another way around this communication block. I get this is tough, but swallow that pride, summarise your perspective, validate that their point of view is different from yours and ask how they propose you both move on considering those differences? Take a break and when you return to the negotiation summarise all the key points so far and ask, "What would need to happen for you to increase volume?" or suggest scenarios such as "allow us to pitch for other products/services" or "What if we could deliver ahead of your time constraints" or "In which circumstances *'would you'* reconsider the price point" etc.

So, back to preparation and planning, once you have listed your variables along the range from **Utopia** to **No-Go** you now need to cost out each movement. You need to be on top of how much every movement is costing you to avoid mistakes. E.g. Payment terms; my **Utopia** might be 90 days; my *likely* position might be 60 days and my **No-Go** position sub 30 days (Let's say a move from 60 to 30 days costs around 1% of total contract value). I need to

The little book of Negotiation Brilliance

calculate each step to ensure my finger is on the pulse every time I move and therefore I can get back in return a variable of similar cost guaranteeing my organisation is securing a good deal without compromising the relationship with the other party (they get what they want but on my terms).

Another tip in preparation and planning is; always know how much the total deal is worth when movement takes place. If there are many changes and you feel like you are trying to keep a tally on the movement of mercury running away from you during the negotiation simply take a break, get out of the room and DO YOUR SUMS, GET CLARITY OF WHERE YOU ARE NOW before continuing.

Create a list of some 'minor' variables that you could use in the box below to gain movement in an imminent work Negotiation you are about to enter into. E.g. If you were buying a car your 'minor' variables might be a tank of fuel, sports wheels, panoramic roof, car mats etc. This will create a generic take and give list for you to gain movement in that negotiation. (Take and Give is on purpose and not a mistake). **ALWAYS** take before you give in a negotiation (State your conditions before you make the offer). This keeps the other party listening to what they need to do in order to secure the gain. It also prevents you giving something away without getting anything back in return. Go back to our car example E.g. If you buy a **car** your key variables are probably Price,

The little book of Negotiation Brilliance

Warranty and Trade-In. Those you would plan across the range from *utopia* to *no-go* and cost each movement out. Then we have the smaller 'minor' variables listed above that can secure even more movement such as sports wheels, panoramic roof, heated seats, servicing, fuel and fortnightly valeting. (Yup! I secured fortnightly valeting on my last car which has saved me a fortune in the long run – we'll see more about how this works when we discuss tactics). Once this list is complete (TIP - the more creative and the longer this list is the more movement you will get) you would use your 'takes' if the other party is moving you away from your utopia towards your more realistic target and your 'gives' if you need extra oomph to move them from their utopia to a more realistic point. E.g. **IF YOU** valet this car every 2 weeks (*take/condition*) **I WILL** agree to signing the deal right now (*give/offer*).

The little book of Negotiation Brilliance

The final area on this activity is to answer; What if we hit our **'No-Go'** and walk away? Where will we walk to? This is where you need to prepare for any alternatives. The number of alternatives will be market driven E.g. if you sit in a leverage market from a buyer perspective or an exploitable market from a seller perspective you will have many options and switching from one supplier to another is low cost and relatively straight forward. If you have alternative solutions, keep them to yourself during the negotiation but have confidence that they are there in your back pocket. These are referred to as BATNA'S (Best Alternative to a Negotiated Agreement). BATNA's give you confidence to walk away but are more generally available in lower risk markets.

If preparing and planning to negotiate in a team it is key that each team member is allocated a specific role and that they understand the responsibilities that come with the role. You need to come across as a united front and ensure every member of the team is on the same page. Key roles to be covered are the Lead, the Assistant, the Technical Expert, Legal and an Observer who will be the eyes and ears of anything that is being missed.

The little book of Negotiation Brilliance

STAGE 2 – SET THE STAGE

Stage 2 is where you set the stage for the performance of the negotiation and build rapport. Yes, Negotiation is a performance where we don our cloak and persona in order to secure a great deal. How the stage is set will condition the other party as to how tough or easy this deal is going to be for them to secure and remember people value what they have worked harder for. In your preparation and planning you will have considered how you need to come across in this meeting; It may be focussed on the relationship at a time where you have little power and therefore unable to make demands or, it could be a more task focussed approach where you have the leverage to drive the outcome towards your desired goal i.e. better price, faster delivery, higher quality or added value.   Remember, what you do or don't do and what you say or don't say in the first five minutes of the negotiation will determine the outcome.   You need to start the meeting with a strong conditioning statement which encourages the other party to walk closer to you and not further away. E.g. when I was negotiating a technology solution on behalf of a client based in London there were 3 suppliers in competition with each other, all who wanted to secure the contract.   This was a competitive Negotiation and my client was in a position where the balance of power sat securely with them.   Their opening phrase, which is one of the best I've heard in a competitive market was… "This is your business to win as much as it's your business to lose". This was of course in a private sector competitive market. It worked! The same opening phrase was used on each supplier and it resulted in instant movement from the other party every time.

Collaborative negotiations where the balance of power sits with the other party would warrant a different opening statement. E.g. "Our relationship is key and one that we value highly. We really need to be creative in this meeting as these price increases are simply not sustainable for us as a business. We need to consider areas of cost efficiency; how could you help us with that?" In this example you, as Lead Negotiator, would continue to use each of the key messages as your broken record throughout the meeting reinforcing what's important to you e.g. "unsustainable price increases and the need for cost efficiency exercises".

There are no magic wands here but setting yourselves up to succeed will give you your best chance of successful outcomes, even in scenarios where you have little to no power.

The little book of Negotiation Brilliance

Another conditioning statement comes from your greeting and handshake. There are many handshakes that were designed to showcase your level of power and dominance over the other party e.g.: -
- The left hand further up your opponent's arms whilst shaking with your right hand.
- The pat on the back of the other party as you pull them in closer when shaking their hand.
- The bone crusher where you apply pressure on the other persons hand.

These handshakes maybe more common in politics however, I have experienced them all too frequently in commercial negotiations.   It is transparent and doesn't put you in a favourable light or a good position to secure the best deal unless you are in an overly aggressive market and you have no power, in that case it may intimidate.

The best handshake would be one that positively mirrored the energy of the other party, it should be an opportunity to build rather than destroy rapport before it starts. All that said, within the post COVID-19 environment we find ourselves, the Negotiation greeting will have changed globally. The 'old-fashioned' handshake will become a thing of the past. In the new normal of social distancing the handshake becomes dated and undesirable.   Post pandemic you will need to consider your new greeting and how you deliver a tough, positive but likeable impact within the first few seconds of meeting the other party.

The little book of Negotiation Brilliance

The handshake may be a thing of the past but eye contact, smiling, assertive body language and being presentable remains. The other party will have, what they consider to be, a solid impression of you within the first 10 seconds of meeting and will determine traits such as trustworthiness. In my opinion we can recover from first impressions but that puts us in a weaker position as prevention is better than cure and if we create a likeable although tough first impression from the start then we condition the other party to think we are in control and are a negotiation force to be reckoned with.

The best feedback I could ever wish for from a commercial negotiation would be "I liked and trusted Sue but jeez she negotiates hard to achieve her business objectives" when I hear that it's like music to my ears. I achieved a successful tight rope walk and maintained the right balance from start to finish.

Think of your imminent negotiation and in the box on the next page write yourself a relevant great opening ('conditioning') statement. You will use this to encourage the other party to move closer to your outcomes, set the tone and you will also defer to this statement throughout your negotiation as your 'broken record' technique to gain movement or regain control. This statement is also designed to reinforce your bottom line and key objective throughout the meeting. Refer to examples quoted within this STAGE 2 section as a starter for ten.

STAGE 3 – VALIDATE & QUESTION

So, we now have the start of a plan and have set the scene for our Negotiation to play out. We have our key variables, the cost of each movement and have considered any alternatives to give us the confidence to walk away. Next we need to list at least 10 'open' questions; a more audacious goal would be 20. Write them down on your preparation and planning template and make sure the other party provides clear answers to each.

The little book of Negotiation Brilliance

Example 'open' questions might be: –

- How's business?
- How are you finding the market in these times?
- What's your business strategy for growth?
- What expansion plans do you have?
- How many people do you employ?
- What issues are your currently experiencing? What impact is that having?
- What capacity are you currently running at?
- What are your key drivers?
- Who would look after the account?
- Who are the key decision makers?
- What are your key drivers?
- What's important to you in the outcome of this deal?
- How you can help us to help you?
- Just suppose we could offer you a turnaround time of 24 hours how would that reflect in the price/cost?
- What if we could increase the volume how would that reflect in available discounts?
- What would need to change for us to agree?
- What's your experience in designing this specification?
- Where are your distribution units?
- Who are your top 10 clients?
- Just suppose you were to win this business what number would we be in terms of your top client list?

And the list of questions goes on...

The little book of Negotiation Brilliance

A question I'm asked often when travelling the world Negotiating is When is the right time to put your stake in the ground?   Well, there are two schools of thought here. I would say use both e.g. If you are sure of your ground and know your market inside and out and are in a competitive/tactical Negotiation put your marker down first but start at an inflated **utopia** position.   Also, have a **wow** position which erodes the confidence of the other party and makes them think twice about putting down an inflated starting point.   A case study here would be; when I had a builder in to build an extension on my house, towards the end of the job I had some household items (quite a bit) that I needed disposing of.   Straight away I said, "If you could take this rubbish away, I will give you £50 cash today".   He accepted even though the market rates for such clearance, at the time, was in excess of £100.   Had I started the negotiation with "What would you charge to clear these items?", I would have given him the power to put his stake in the ground first at his inflated price of around £110. He agreed to the £50 which meant we achieved a win-win scenario (he was paid cash up-front on the day and I paid less to have my rubbish removed).   That said, if you are unsure of your market or the power doesn't sit with you there is a need to uncover the 'REAL' bargaining arena (B.A) and you can only do this through intelligent questioning and listening.

The little book of Negotiation Brilliance

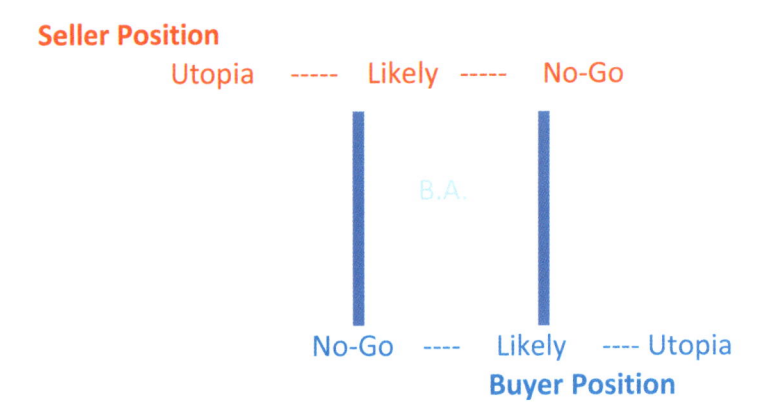

Seller Position
Utopia ----- Likely ----- No-Go

B.A.

No-Go ---- Likely ---- Utopia
Buyer Position

***B**argaining **A**rena (**B.A.**)*

Before reading onto Stage 4 refer back to the earlier questions list and reflect on those that you think might help to uncover the bargaining arena.

The little book of Negotiation Brilliance

If you truly listen and stay 100% present in the conversation the other party will tell you where their markers are and how far they are prepared to move but listening is the master skill here (we'll cover 'signals of movement' later in the book).   Once you think you have the bargaining arena clear in your mind, take a break, draft a proposal starting around their No-Go point.

Remember Negotiation is all about 'MOVEMENT' so be prepared to give a little and get something back in return. The bargaining arena sets out the playing field in which it is sensible to play.   Once you identify *their* 'No-Go's' your area of potential movement sits between that and **your** 'No-Go's' as in the diagram on the previous page.   Of course, some bargaining arenas are wider than depicted in the illustration above with more room for movement and some less.   Other bargaining arenas may display no room for movement and in those cases, you would need to defer to your BATNA.

When preparing and planning you set *your* objectives but also consider the Utopia, Likely and No-Go positions of the other party.   You make assumptions on their position and then check those out during the **validate and question** stage of the negotiation.   In order to check out any assumptions you have made add more questions to your previous list which looks to achieve 2 things;

The little book of Negotiation Brilliance

1) unveil where their markers are set
2) identify where movement is likely to come from

Examples of questions that uncover the other party's markers.
- What do you need to achieve from today's meeting?
- What are your key drivers?
- What do we need to do in order to secure a deal today?
- What is your magic number for agreement?
- What do you consider to be a fair price?
- What is your budget?
- What are your projections for the next 12 months?
- Which elements are you prepared to move on?

We cover tactics later but a key tactic in this **validate and question** stage is to recap and summarise regularly. Summarising will help to maintain control and keep the negotiation focussed and on track. Summarising will prevent you buying the wrong bridge E.g. Back in 1967 Robert McCulloh wanted to buy a bridge from London to improve tourism around Lake Havasu City, Arizona. The story leads us to believe that Robert McCulloh thought he was buying the ornate and fabulous Tower Bridge however when the bridge arrived in America, he realised it was 'just a bridge' yup! That's London Bridge Mr M, that's what you said. (Most tourists refer to Tower Bridge as London Bridge. To the Brits they are two very different constructions). Had Robert McCulloh summarised effectively this mistake would never have happened; he may never have secured a sale of Tower Bridge but at least he would know what he was taking delivery of or indeed he would have had the opportunity to change his mind and walk away.

STAGE 4 – TRADE

This is a critical phase of the Negotiation as this is where you start moving and each movement is at a cost to your organisation and to the overall deal. Your key objective within the **Trade** phase is to stay 100% present and listen. Complete the box below and list the things skilled negotiators need to listen for when Negotiating.

The little book of Negotiation Brilliance

Your list will be a combination of many things I'm sure. At this phase you are specifically listening for signals of movement. Our brains are wired to listen for numbers during a Negotiation and the number tells you zilch! How would you know whether the number they quote right now is their **Utopia, Likely or No-Go** target? It's the pre-cursor that comes before the number that's key. The "approximately" "something like" "round about" "we're looking for". These signals tell you loud and clear there is movement available. The good news for you as a negotiator is these signals are instinctive human behaviour and even the best negotiators struggle to keep them hidden. The bad news I'm afraid, is that you will be using them too. So, we need to listen to the pre-cursors of the other party and practice and rehearse as much as possible to ensure we limit the times we give signals from our side.

When the other party concedes (even if they didn't mean to) thank them and show appreciation immediately. You then take ownership of what has been offered, no matter how small their concession. Even if you think it's a variable of no or limited use to you still take ownership. This will keep the other party giving and will get you a little closer to your goals. E.g. It took the sales lady 4 months to get me to commit to buying my 'new build' house. Sarah (the sales lady) offered, quite early on, a voucher to help towards my solicitor's fees. (Caveat; the small print stated this £500 voucher was only to be used with the building company's preferred solicitor and that it was only

The little book of Negotiation Brilliance

valid for a limited period). On the face of it I knew the voucher, in reality wasn't worth very much. However, at the time, I thanked Sarah for the concession and took ownership of said voucher. Once we were at the final stages and close to me signing on the dotted line I said "Sarah, you kindly gave me a voucher towards my solicitors fees which you stated had a value of £500. I have been very fortunate to have a solicitor friend that has agreed to manage all of my conveyancing activities however, I am conscious that you mentioned these vouchers are rare and not often given to clients i.e. they are pretty hard to come by. Sarah, if you reduce the remaining price of the property by £500, I will sign the contract now and give you the valuable voucher back which will help one of your other clients". She agreed.

The moral of that story being…Had I rejected the variable (in this case the voucher) as it wasn't of any value to me, I would have missed out on the final small movement at the end of the negotiation. If you are looking for a 5% discount and the other party offers you 0.25%, show your appreciation for that movement but keep your foot on the accelerator, keep them building on that momentum of small movements until you get closer to your desired target and accept anything that will give you leverage later on. This is the 'Oliver' tactic – "please sir can I have more". You leave it until the end of the negotiation, these are small requests that add extra value to your overall deal. E.g. "I'm delighted we are almost at an

The little book of Negotiation Brilliance

agreement, just to clarify that will of course include postage…. won't it?" More on tactics later, how to use them and more importantly how to recognise and counter tactics being used by the other party on you.

You need power in the **trade** phase of a negotiation so where does power come from? List your thoughts in the box below, think of people who you negotiate with and consider what is the source of their power. Then check your list against mine on the next page.

The little book of Negotiation Brilliance

- Time can give you power
- Information, Legitimate market position and authority all give you power
- BATNA's give you the power/confidence to walk away
- Your beliefs. E.g. If you believe you have power your presence will ooze personal power
- Body language – Be upright, stay engaged through eye contact, be animated when expressing your points
- Your greeting and first impressions give an instant perception of personal power

We'll discuss power again and in more detail in the 'Gaining Movement' section later in the book.

STAGE 5 – CLOSE OUT

At this stage both parties know where they are. The deal on the table is transparent and understood by all. The key task here is to ensure that you summarise the deal for the final time and agree the detail. What you do or don't do at this stage could affect the setting up and implementation of any contract that follows. Summaries add clarity, should be fact based and devoid of any opinion or view. A summary is simply a stock take of what has been agreed on both sides.

The little book of Negotiation Brilliance

If you are walking away from a deal at this point do so with a personable approach as revenge may be sweet if the other party feels cheated or let down professionally but also, unless you are a fortune teller, you don't know what the future holds and it would be a tough day if you had to return to that same person to reignite business discussions at a later date.

STAGE 6 – REVIEW
The review stage happens outside of the Negotiation meeting. This is about continuous improvement, growth and development. This stage is about you, your team and your organisation raising the bar on Negotiation capability. You must measure the outcome against your originally planned **Utopia – Likely – No-Go** targets. Which variables did you agree at a Utopia level? On reflection were those targets stretched or could they have been tougher? Which variables did you walk away from, those that hit your **No-Go** point? How creative were you and your team? What tactics worked well? What did you give away without getting anything back in return? (I would hope you answer 'nothing' to this question ☺).

In summary this stage is about identifying what successes and challenges you had and what you would do differently next time. You then create an action plan to ensure the reflections are fed back into your next Negotiation plan and that best practice is shared within your team and the wider organisation. Oh! And get out there and celebrate those successes.

The little book of Negotiation Brilliance

ROLLING THE DICE
Tactics we deploy and techniques for recognising and countering tactics used by the other party

Tactics are discreet activities that are injected within each stage of the Negotiation process. Tactics are used to achieve 1 of four things: -
1) Break the 'NO'
2) Create movement
3) Regain control
4) Delay responses

The above 4 points have many tactics that achieve their objective but one tactic that fits with all of the above is –

Summarise! Summarise! Summarise! Summarise! Summarise! She shouts from the rooftops as loud as she possibly can. Summaries are THE most powerful tool in your armoury of Negotiation skills, let me explain; Summaries help to control all types of negotiation; they bring any forgotten variables back onto the table, they diffuse any heated arguments if tempers are starting to bubble up and they make space for you (as Lead Negotiator) to think especially if you have an Assistant that has the responsibility for summarising.

The little book of Negotiation Brilliance

'ALWAYS' maintain control of summaries and never give away an opportunity to Summarise. If you allow the other party to summarise you hand them control at the same time.

One dictionary definition of Tactics is; **skilful actions to achieve a goal. Are they skilful actions or, is the whole thing just a game to get what you want?**

There is a ritual to negotiation which most people see as a game. If you offer me £300,000 for a house that I'm trying to sell for £395,000 and I accept the offer immediately, how would you feel? Cheated? disappointed? Whatever the feeling, you will think you could have done better and feel less happy with the outcome. The game/ritual wasn't played out, I conceded too quickly. However, if you make the same offer which we discuss at length, both move slowly over a few days or weeks, show creativity and add in extras e.g. window blinds, white goods, light fittings, whilst using a range of tactics, and eventually we agree to just over your offer of £315,000, you walk away feeling much more positive and pleased with the deal. People value what they have worked harder for. There is a psychology to the 'game' of negotiation, a culture, a tradition with lots of complex manoeuvres. Only once the game has been played out skilfully will each party feel good about the outcome.

The little book of Negotiation Brilliance

There is plethora of tactics to help us achieve success in negotiation, some of which you will feel comfortable using and others you may feel are under-handed, even unthinkable. However, don't be fooled that others wouldn't use them on you! The application of tactics requires confidence, you have to plan your strategy and within that select the right tactics for the right people in the right market.

How we deploy our tactics is only one half of the coin, we need to understand and recognise tactics being used by the other party. Once you recognise tactics coming from the other side of the table, and have the ability to label them as such, it will reduce the impact they have on you and ultimately the deal. It will also arm you with the skills to counter those tactics effectively and therefore won't result in stopping you in your tracks and smashing straight into a stalemate situation.

When preparing and planning for negotiations it is imperative that due consideration is given to the market in which you are operating in, as this will determine the approach required e.g. competitive, collaborative or co-operative. There are 2 main categories of negotiation approach: competitive and collaborative.

The little book of Negotiation Brilliance

You might use silence to exert pressure in a competitive negotiation but the use of this tactic in a collaborative situation could damage the relationship. On the other hand, you might use the 'open hand' tactic in a collaborative negotiation but this would be foolhardy in a competitive situation. Use the right tactic for the right market at the right time.

KEEPING THE OTHER PARTY ON THEIR TOES
You need a plethora of different tactics in your negotiation toolkit as this enables you to be unpredictable. In the words of the great Henry Ford "If you always do what you've always done, you'll always get what you've always got". For example, sometime ago I came across a formidable Union representative who was known for getting what he wanted out of most negotiations. He was about to embark on a negotiation regarding new start and finish times on a factory floor and decided to take his right-hand man into the Negotiation to assist him. His brief to his colleague was 'Once we have presented our proposal, we will use silence and put the pressure on. Do not speak at that point'. This he did and the silence lasted for a solid 5 minutes which felt like a lifetime. It worked! The employers acquiesced and the Union representative and his assistant secured a good deal for the workers. However, a year later a very similar negotiation had to be undertaken with the same employers and the rep and his assistant adopted the same strategy. This time however the employers had planned for the silence which they

The little book of Negotiation Brilliance

managed to counter with matching the silent 5-minute period. So, the moral of the story is...stay clear of being predictable otherwise you will get caught out and use the right tactic at the right time.

Negotiation is a skill that can be learned and practised. That said, we need a broad variety of tactics to support us when times get tough, when we need to regain control, create movement, delay responses or break the 'NO'.

The following includes some of my favourite 'go-to' tactics.

The Steppingstone: designed to create movement. If you came across a stream it is unlikely you would jump from one side to the other without getting your feet wet so you would step onto the first stone, then the second and so on until you reach the other side. This same approach works in commercial negotiations. E.g. If you are prepared to enter into a 3-year contract, negotiate hard for year one and then ask what they would offer in addition if you were in a position to go to two years. Having obtained further concessions, test the water with "(*Just suppose*...) we could offer three years". For each steppingstone you will secure more movement and be offered more concessions. (On the other hand, if you start your discussion and give your 3-year marker upfront and in full you will only secure 1 movement/concession and will lose out on the incremental build up).

The little book of Negotiation Brilliance

Break-off: When technical data or lots of different figures, cost models, pricing strategies, exchange rates are flying about take a **break-off** to review, recalculate, be creative or even decide how to match the information overload from the other party.

This will slow down the pace of the negotiation and help to get you back into a position of power and authority. However, before calling the **break-off** it is critical that you summarise the discussion so far. As mentioned before summaries are an excellent tactic as they can bring concessions back onto the table that may otherwise be lost, reduce the temperature of any conflict and clarify understanding whilst buying you time to think. Never leave or restart a meeting without a summary, its key to ensure both parties are on the same page in terms of movement and achievements so far. Plus, it prevents a London Bridge vs Tower Bridge scenario.

Parking: If you are on the receiving end of tough demands from the other party that you are unable to match or the other party is raising minor issues to take you off track or even throwing in unexpected topics for discussion then **park** those issues for now. Regain control and come back to their point later, once you have had a chance to plan any changes to your movement strategy.   If the other party has a different focus in terms of what is key in the negotiation give them confidence that this is absolutely important to you too and you will come back to it. You can postpone for 10 minutes, 30 minutes, 2 hours or a few days. The **parking** technique helps you to plan for anything unexpected that is raised during the negotiation – you need time to respond rather than react from a knee jerk position.

Open Hand: This tactic is one that is used in Collaborative negotiations where you have less power than the other party. In order to create an environment of trust and openness you approach the negotiation from an 'open book' point of view. You might divulge financial information, technical information, growth plans etc early on in the meeting with the hope they will match the information but also with the objective in mind to showcase yourselves as a potential partner who demonstrates integrity, openness and honesty at all times. This open disclosure approach is kept for those relationships that are key to your organisation.

Oliver: this tactic is used in a more competitive environment where you are trying to secure 'even more' movement at the end of the meeting just before you sign on the dotted line. You might pick up your pen to sign and just before you do you suggest that you would like more please sir/madam! "Just before I sign, this will include a testimonial on our website…. won't it?". The other party will often capitulate and accept rather than re-open the negotiation.

The little book of Negotiation Brilliance

Commonly used 'tricks'

Good cop bad cop: Used often, and a tactic I come across regularly. In my opinion it is less effective than you may think. It is transparent! It has been overused! It is theatrical! And there are other more sophisticated tactics that maintain rapport and achieve the same objective as 'Good cop bad cop'. That said, people still use this approach on me and because it is so transparent it is one of the easiest tactics to recognise and therefore counter. The counter to this tactic is 'Divide and Conquer' which means you essentially play one off against the other. E.g. I was involved in a Negotiation on behalf of an Oil and Gas client based in Russia. Leaving the cultural aspects to one side the other party pretty much played 'Good cop Bad cop' throughout every meeting. Their approach was fairly aggressive and the team I was leading were a little rattled by the approach as the outcome of the deal was important to their business. As the other party's approach was obvious, I briefed the team to let it play out until we had engineered a deeper level of rapport. Once that was securely in place, I coached my team to maintain eye contact only with Good cop, nodding, showing empathy and a real interest in the facts he was presenting. He slowly became totally engaged in only our conversation and was singing like a small morning bird and divulging more than his Bad cop partner deemed reasonable. From our peripheral vision we noticed the bad cop beginning to grimace, fidget, stiffen up and become increasingly agitated. We then summarised all the information we had just been given, maintaining eye contact with Bad cop only, then offered the partners a **break-off** to consider where we should go next. The Divide and Conquer counter often causes decent amongst the ranks of the other party, so it is only fair to offer a recess for them to regroup. Once we restarted the tone was more conciliatory and amenable and that was the end of the Good cop bad cop approach.

Remember when selecting tactics:
- What will work in a positive way with one person could equally have a negative impact with another

- Every negotiation is different, and you will need to consider which tactics are appropriate for which markets

In the box on the next page list any tactics you have used in the past or currently use and any tactics that have been used on you. Once you have recorded each tactic check them against the table that follows and then add any others that you feel would be useful in an imminent negotiation you are about to enter into. The table lists 5 of the more common Tactics you may use, their descriptions and how you might counter each tactic if used by the other party.

The little book of Negotiation Brilliance

The little book of Negotiation Brilliance

The following table lists the tactic, the description and then how you would counter that tactic if used on you by the other party.

TACTIC	DESCRIPTION	COUNTER
Silence	This is different to being attentive and listening. Silence as a tactic is used after you present your proposal. You present your proposal stating your conditions and the offer (IF YOU …. THEN I'LL), you then invite a response from the other party. Then you 'zip' you do not say a word. Stay silent until they speak.	The first person to break a silence generally concedes. Remain silent and the other party will start to unpick their proposal and probably start to move away from their initial targets. If you feel uncomfortable, summarise the key points of the proposal and call a break-off. When you come back present your counter proposal.
Data fog	This is where you invite your technical experts to attend the negotiation and blind the other party with science. It can also be used as a **'Snowstorm'** a deluge of information delivered in one go which can cause confusion for the other party.	Stay 100% present and listen to the information. Capture notes on areas you need to clarify. When the other party finishes what they are saying ask your questions and stay persistent until you have clarity. This approach will slow the negotiation pace, drill into the detail and ensure you understand before moving on. Once your questions are answered summarise and **break-off**. Invite your own technical expert at this point if required.

The little book of Negotiation Brilliance

The choice	This tactic offers 2 possibilities e.g. we agree to A or B? It reduces an endless list of possible options and drives agreement towards the two you would prefer. E.g. Either I can reduce the price by 1% or I can extend our payment terms. Which would you prefer? You can make **The Choice** more aggressive by making 1 of the options more palatable than the other which forces the other party to choose the one option you prefer. E.g. We can deliver today at the premium rate before the winter roads start to melt or we can reduce the price significantly but probably miss your very tight delivery slot. Which would you prefer? *(scenario refers to an Oil & Gas Negotiation I was involved in when negotiating in Siberia)*	Firstly, show your appreciation for the options presented. Take a break-off giving yourself time to think each option through; the benefits, the drawbacks and any other possibilities. Return to the Negotiation with your suggestions, present them and then use silence until the other party responds.
Corridor	This tactic is a side conversation that happens during a '**break-off**' called by the other party. The objective is to catch you off guard outside the Negotiating room when the pressure is off. It will be disguised as "How do you think things are progressing?" "I noticed some tension earlier is everything ok?"	Stay alert to informal conversations with the other party during a 'break-off'. If approached whilst in a relaxed state either change the subject to some small talk (chit chat) or say, let's discuss in more detail when we start again after our recess.
Package	This is where the other party	Cut their pie into slices and

The little book of Negotiation Brilliance

Pie	packages you in a deal. It sounds similar to a summary; the other party lists several variables and then presents the discount available. E.g. For a 2-year agreement, 10,000 units a year, 30-day payment terms, joint advertising, quarterly batch deliveries and our partnership advertised on both websites we will offer you a 2.5% discount on current prices.	after every slice question the associated value in terms of discount. Keep your foot on the accelerator until every variable has been agreed. This takes patience, confidence and focus. At the end you will have achieved a number greater than the original 2.5% offered. E.g. What value have they associated with each piece of the pie. Each element should produce movement.

The little book of Negotiation Brilliance

GAINING MOVEMENT; ZERO POWER & MONOPOLY SITUATIONS
Influencing and Persuading others when you have little to no power

Sometimes we are in a position where we have little to no power and to make things worse the other party knows that too. Sometimes we are undermined by the people above us in our own company hierarchy, they may have an existing relationship with the other party and have suggested the deal is won but the finite details just need to be sorted with Procurement or Sales (whichever department you represent). Other times it's a legitimate market dynamic that puts us in a position of zero power e.g. from a procurement point of view Monopoly or Duopoly suppliers. From a Sales point of view those customers that are critical to your business success. Whatever the reason, it can feel like you are negotiating with your hands tied behind your back at times. So, what to do!

A topical situation in today's COVID-19 environment is the communication method we might choose to hold our Negotiation meetings. Face to face is fast becoming a rarity where you can see what's behind the eyes of the other party, you can study facial expressions and identify pacifying body language movements more closely. We are moving to a new norm of virtual meetings such as

The little book of Negotiation Brilliance

video conferencing, teleconferences, Zoom, Skype for business, Microsoft Teams etc. In such technically driven scenarios, we need to focus on how we increase our personal power, impact and presence to demonstrate confidence in our Negotiations.

Personal power is about perception, and your presence adds to the power you are perceived as having by the other party. An important footnote here is that body language does not disappear over the phone, remember whatever you do with your physiology affects your state of mind at that time. This is why people are trained to stand in call centres when dealing with difficult and challenging customers. To influence and persuade we need impact, gravitas, a strong presence and power, all of which is judged from our body language and the way we present ourselves.

John French and Bertram Raven (1959) were social psychologists who studied power. The study tells us that power is divided into five separate and distinct forms. They tell us that power comes from five bases;

- **coercive** - the power to remove
- **reward** – the power to award
- **legitimate** – the power of position in either the market or the hierarchy
- **referent** – the power to be liked and to rally the troops either as enablers or blockers
- **expert** – the power of being a subject matter expert e.g. technical, legal, product knowledge

The little book of Negotiation Brilliance

Check back on your reflection box within the TRADE stage section where you listed your thoughts on where power comes from. Now annotate that list with the above sources of power in order to identify who has what source and level of power within your Negotiations.

It is important to understand what power we and the other party have, the source of that power and how effective it is being applied throughout Negotiations. E.g. It is common knowledge that some of the big corporate giants out there have exerted their legitimate power in a way that smaller companies have viewed as an abuse of power, through making unachievable demands or showing a complete lack of empathy and co-operation. It's not that they used their power it's more about **how** they used it.

Power and the ability to influence generally falls into two categories; Personal Power or Positional Power.
Power in a Negotiation also comes from being well prepared, rehearsing and running simulations with your team for big ticket negotiations. E.g. I work with a selection of clients that use my services simply to get themselves 'Negotiation Fit' for those high risk/high spend supplier Negotiations and key account/high value customer negotiations. I work closely with the team and every day we run through their preparation progress and then we rehearse the actual negotiation using live data and record each section of that Negotiation. We sit together and playback every recording and critique each

The little book of Negotiation Brilliance

step. It's similar to an athlete getting ready for their performance on the world stage for an Olympic event; practice, practice and more practice. Athletes run recordings of the race through their minds at every opportunity and they keep re-running the recording until there are no mistakes. They know every lump, bump, turn and stone on the course and their confidence is high on race day. They know 'they've got this'. When negotiating on complex global deals it is imperative that every member of your team is 'Negotiation Fit' and all on the same page. Confidence gives you power.

The little book of Negotiation Brilliance

MOVEMENT STRATEGY AND GETTING PEOPLE TO 'AGREEMENT'

Source: Robert Cialdini, President of INFLUENCE AT WORK
(influenceatwork.com)

Once you have analysed your source and level of power you now need to apply them and, as you can't 'tell' anyone to move in a negotiation, you need to influence like your life depends on it. You need to get the other party to 'AGREEMENT'.

Dr Cialdini is Regents' Professor Emeritus of Psychology and Marketing at Arizona State University. He is the author of the New York Times Bestseller, *Influence*, which has sold 5 million copies in 41 languages (a great piece of work that I highly recommend). Robert Cialdini developed the six universal Principles of Persuasion. These six powerful tools are: Reciprocity, Commitment & Consistency, Social Proof, Authority, Liking and Scarcity.

- **Reciprocity** – At first sight this might seem like a cardinal sin in Negotiation as you need to give something up early in the meeting... Act first! This is on the basis that humans hate to feel indebted to others. E.g. When a friend offers to babysit your kids, you have a great night out and when you return home your parting words to your friend are

The little book of Negotiation Brilliance

"We will return the favour, just let us know when". Or after a dinner party, as you're leaving, you feel obliged to say, "You must come to us next time". Your friend and dinner party host gave something, and we feel obliged to '**reciprocate**'.

- **Commitment & Consistency** – The scientific research on Commitment and Consistency shows that people want to be consistent with what they have previously said or done. So, when developing your proposal, be sure to align parts of it to what the other party has already committed to. E.g. cost efficiency, rapid turnaround or environmentally friendly aspects. Just before presenting your proposal, let your client know that you realise how important 'x' is to them, so you have developed your proposal to feature that. The other party will feel an extra pull to be consistent with what they have already said or done that is reflected in your proposal. Also remember people live up to what they write down so, summarise on flipchart or whiteboard and invite signatures and the other party will remain consistent and committed to what was agreed after the meeting.

The little book of Negotiation Brilliance

- **Social Proof** – People take confidence from others. Leverage testimonials and use the right language. Think of Social Proof as people power. So, if you have testimonials about yourself, your company and prior success of your company, be sure your client sees those before they see your proposal. For example, if you are negotiating with a pharmaceutical company, before receiving your proposal, make sure the other party sees testimonials from other pharmaceutical clients. If you are negotiating with a financial services company, be sure your client has already seen how successful your negotiation was with other financial services companies. With Social Proof, the more similar the testimonials are to the other party, and the more of them, the more effective Social Proof will be.

- **Liking** – It's important to find out what you have in common with the other party and to bring that to the surface before you start your negotiations. The more "core" those similarities are, the better. So, if you find out that you are both passionate about animals, make sure that the other party knows about that. It will lead to them liking you more AND importantly, it will lead you to liking them more as well.

The little book of Negotiation Brilliance

- **Authority** – Demonstrate your genuine expertise. It's important to understand that Authority is not referring to "in authority", but to being "an authority". So, if you have expertise in a relevant area, make sure the other party knows of your relevant degrees, awards, or certifications in those areas.

- **Scarcity** – When considering Scarcity, highlight what is rare or dwindling in availability in your proposal. People are motivated by the thought of loss rather than gaining that same thing. Yes, present the benefits of working with your company, but also include what is unique to your company. Or, present a unique combination of traits that your proposal and/or your company has. Remember that these all need to be honest.

Final note on Power and influence and, I guess, a word of caution. When you hit the **'trade'** stage in the negotiation process it is especially key that you don't erode the power you have, the momentum you have built and the credibility you have set by moving too quickly and in movements that are too good to be true. This will not motivate the other party; it has the opposite effect! If you move in chunks that are deemed as too big the other party will lose faith in your starting point. Remember, people value what they work harder for. Move slowly and in small steps and stay persistent until you reach your desired target.   As you **'close-out'** you may need to compromise on any final variables. It's worth remembering that a 'mid-way split' is a weak starting position in a compromise situation. If you are negotiating with a skilled negotiator, they will keep their foot on the accelerator and push you further which could leave you at 40% and them at 60%.   A compromise is a movement that focuses on a single variable. E.g. if I share my water with you, I will start by giving you a small glass and I keep the rest. The moral of the story is start high (70 or 80% in your favour) and let the other party push you towards the mid-way. At least then you have definitely secured 50%. Maintain the power and keep your foot on the accelerator until the very end of the Negotiation.

The little book of Negotiation Brilliance

MAGIC WANDS AND STAYING 100% PRESENT
Be an Emotionally Intelligent negotiator

We spoke earlier about walking the tight rope of negotiations where we stay engaged on a personal level with the other party without compromising on our business issues, goals and objectives. Being a hard negotiator can be short lived when relationships are important, as revenge is sweet, and if you drill the other party down to their bare minimum today, they will get you or your organisation back at some point in the future. Remember; If I *like* you and I have more legitimate power in the negotiation I am more likely to give you some of what I have but if I *dislike* you, I am more likely to focus only on my own gains. For example: When teenagers demand £10 to go into town on a Saturday and get into a strop if asked to do a few jobs around the house to earn the money and that strop escalates into them storming off and slamming their door, you are more likely to retract the £10 and give nothing. However, if the teenager asks in a way that is respectful, agrees or even offers to do something in return such as pick you up some shopping whilst they're out and show their appreciation, you are more likely to hand over the money and if a softie with your kids (like me) they might tug at your emotional strings and you end up giving more.

The little book of Negotiation Brilliance

So, the Emotionally Intelligent Negotiator has the balance between being persistent and focussed on their own goals and remaining approachable and likeable during the negotiation. This means they build rapport, maintain rapport and sometimes break rapport when the strategy requires that to happen. As I mentioned earlier, the feedback I aim for after every negotiation (no matter what market I am operating in) is "I like Sue but boy is she tough to Negotiate with". Every time I receive this feedback, I know I hit the nail on the head in terms of that tight rope walk throughout the Negotiation. I also know that I demonstrated emotional intelligence throughout to build and maintain the relationship.

There are 4 pillars to Emotional Intelligence which are: -

Self-awareness – Knowing your own emotions, strengths and weaknesses and recognising their impact. Having self-confidence and a positive sense of self-worth.

Social-awareness – Having the ability to show empathy and read the emotions and feelings of others. Taking an interest in the other party and their goals and aspirations. Being sensitive and adaptable to the reactions of others.

The little book of Negotiation Brilliance

Self-management – Knowing your own hot buttons and instances that make you react. Having an internal toolkit to manage yourself and respond appropriately. Displaying honesty, integrity and adjusting to changing situations when overcoming obstacles. Being motivated to achieve and seize opportunities.

Relationship-management – the ability to communicate in a way the other party understands. To stay 100% present in conversations with the other party (active listening). The ability to build and maintain relationships with collaboration and promote co-operation.

Emotionally intelligent (Ei) Negotiators consistently leave a positive impact on others, they persuade and influence key stakeholders, suppliers, customers, family, friends and colleagues. The most powerful method of persuasion is to articulate how you feel in a Negotiation e.g. joy, disappointment, excitement, concern, let down, happy, sad, frustrated. If you are disappointed in the offer presented by the other party, you need to flag that disappointment followed by silence. Emotionally intelligent negotiators do not jump in immediately to justify why they are disappointed as the other party will simply argue with the logic as they will have their own perception of the facts. State your disappointment, hold

The little book of Negotiation Brilliance

your silence for a few seconds and ask your next question or invite a response to your proposal.

Emotionally intelligent Negotiators are mindful of their impact at all times. What they are saying, how they are saying it and whether their body language and posture supports that message. As a cross check consider whether what you are saying is congruent with the tone and your body language. Your body language and tone have the most impact on the other party. E.g. I can call my kids down from their Playstation or X box for dinner in a maternal caring tone but if I've called them several times with no results my words remain the same, but my body language and tone become agitated, frustrated, irritated and at times aggressive. Remember the old adage? "It's not what you said, it's the way you said it". Emotionally intelligent Negotiators are cognisant throughout the meetings and stay 100% present, reading the other party's tone and body language whilst being mindful of their own impact and the signals they may be sending out.

The little book of Negotiation Brilliance

Listening is the Master Skill of Emotionally intelligent Negotiators. I don't just mean 'active' listening I mean staying 100% present in the conversation – Ei negotiators speak 20% of the time (when asking great questions) and listen 80% of the time. Hand on heart when you are negotiating are you *really* listening to the other party or are you waiting for the gap in the conversation when you can next speak? Are you listening in your own head to your own agenda? Are you planning your response or your next question? Food for thought! People pay good money to be listened too. The deeper the rapport the better the outcome you will secure and staying 100% interested in the other party will build that deep level of rapport.

The little book of Negotiation Brilliance

TOOLKIT SUMMARY ARTICLES & TAKEAWAY'S

THE 'ONE PAGE' TEAM DOCUMENT

A useful tool in any team negotiation is a document that ensures any potential information leaks are managed. This document would usually be used in big ticket negotiations, it is an internal document which is completed with cross functional teams and distributed to your negotiation team, your internal stakeholders and anyone within your business that is likely to engage in dialogue with a potential supplier or customer. We need to ensure we all sing from the same song sheet and come across as a united front rather than undermining each other's positions by giving away key information. Used effectively this document gives the team strength and power in complex negotiations.

Complete the box below with how you currently guarantee that each member of your team is drip feeding the right amount and right quality of information at any touch point with the other party.

The little book of Negotiation Brilliance

In my experience when Negotiating in teams this is an incredibly valuable tool. It was shared with me many years ago by one of my mentors and I have used it ever since.

This internal document ensures consistent messaging around several areas such as the overall aim of the negotiation, the conditioning statement and the broken record messaging tactic. It lists information that anyone is free to discuss outside of the negotiation meeting and also lists information the team should avoid discussing directly with the other party. The document below is an example with generic suggestions on how it might be used.

The little book of Negotiation Brilliance

THE 'ONE PAGE' TEAM DOCUMENT

Negotiation: **Date:**
Team Members:

- Overall Aim/objective of the Negotiation

  - Secure a key account
  - Drive for profit
  - Review performance

- Key conditioning statement to manage the other party's expectations

  - Under extreme cost pressure
  - The struggle in this market is REAL and is driven by the volatility in price

- Green Light Information 'Gives'

  - Relationship is key
  - We have the technical expertise
  - Need to engage with the right suppliers,

- Red light Information 'Nevers'

  - Commercials - Costs, Pricing, Budget
  - Length of contract
  - Technical specifications
  - Our weaknesses

The little book of Negotiation Brilliance

OVER TO YOU

Below prepare a 'one-page team document' with an upcoming Team Negotiation in mind.

'ONE PAGE' TEAM DOCUMENT

Negotiation: Date:
Team Members:

➡ Overall Aim/objective of the Negotiation

➡ Key conditioning statement to manage the other party expectations

➡ Green Light Information 'Gives'

➡ Red Light Information 'Nevers'

The little book of Negotiation Brilliance

As we approach the end of the Little Book of Negotiation Brilliance let's take some time out for self-reflection. Answer the following questions as you would have done before reading this book, go with your gut reactions.

- How often do you plan 'well' for a Negotiation?
    - a) Always
    - b) Sometimes
    - c) Only when time allows
    - d) Never

- When have you used a BATNA in the past?
    - a) Always
    - b) Sometimes
    - c) Only when time allows
    - d) Never

- Have you used summaries to control your negotiations?
    - a) Yes
    - b) No
    - c) Sometimes
    - d) Don't know

The little book of Negotiation Brilliance

- How often do you ask closed questions instead of open?
    - a) Always
    - b) Sometimes
    - c) When I remember
    - d) Never

- How confident do you feel when negotiating?
    - a) Totally
    - b) Somewhat
    - c) It depends who I am negotiating with
    - d) Not at all

Now answer them again with your new knowledge from this book. Have your answers changed and if so, consider what changes you might make to your next 'REAL' Negotiation.

The little book of Negotiation Brilliance

NEGOTIATION PLAN
(APPENDIX 1)

Supplier: Negotiation date:

Major Issues	UTOPIA	U-L (£)	LIKELY	L-N (£)	NO-GO

The little book of Negotiation Brilliance

TAKE	GIVE

The little book of Negotiation Brilliance

Record any barriers to creating value and strategies for overcoming those barriers

Expected Barriers	Strategies to overcome each barrier

The little book of Negotiation Brilliance

Who's involved?

Key Stakeholder (Ours)	Our Objectives	Key stakeholders (Theirs)	Their Objectives

The little book of Negotiation Brilliance

Movement strategies

Method	Our strategy	Their strategy	Our counter
Compelling Arguments			
Coercion/threats			
Trades			
Final haggles to gain agreement			

The little book of Negotiation Brilliance

Other areas to consider for preparation:

- Which market are we in? What strategy does this require? E.g. Is this a high risk and high profit item or does this fall into a low risk high profit item. This will determine your approach and therefore help to build your strategy.
- What tactics will we use? What tactics might they use and how will we counter each?
- Do we have a BATNA? Can we walk away?
- What are the profiles of each member of the other Negotiation team? How should I communicate to get the best out of them?
- How creative are we being in terms of variables within this Negotiation? Care not to only focus on the regular variable such as price, length of contract, delivery and quality. What else can you offer that would be of value to them but little cost to you?
- What questions do you need to ask the other party in order to understand their position in detail? Ensure your questions are open, that you listen and respond to their points and remember the "Under what circumstances can you…." When you hit a potential stalemate

The little book of Negotiation Brilliance

- If you are approaching this as a team, consider how you have briefed each member of your team. Allocate specific roles and responsibilities.
- Consider the mode of communication you will use in these times of COVID and social distancing. Telephone, Teleconference, face to face and consider your own personal impact.
- Be mindful of the cost to your business of every move you make towards the other party e.g. if you increase volume how much has that just added onto the total value etc.

FINALLY! - What will you say within the first 5 minutes to condition the other party to move towards your objectives. Remember this statement is incredibly powerful and can be used throughout the Negotiation as your bottom-line statement.   Record your statement in the box below and share with all team members using the 'One Page' team document.

The little book of Negotiation Brilliance

(ARTICLE - APPENDIX 2)
PREPARATION & PLANNING FOR THOSE WHO ARE TIME STARVED

Time starved? Negotiating in a hurry? No time to prepare? … sounds like the real world to me. This article will provide some practical Do's and Don'ts which give you more than half a chance of driving success even in time starved environments and may make the difference between success or failure in your next negotiation. There is an emergency kit for those who are really up against it and about to enter a Negotiation that is reactionary rather than well planned and thought through. However, if the Negotiation is important, high risk, high value or core to your business then you must *postpone*.

- Do be clear about your WHY? – Why am I negotiating? What are the goals, aims, objectives and variables? You need clarity and a clear focus when time starved. In a competitive market, know what you want and keep your eye on the prize. Know your market and put 'your' marker down early to set the expectation of the other party. Time is of the essence, so you need to know quickly if the other party is not going to be able to deliver to your specification and price point. This allows you to move on to another option.

The little book of Negotiation Brilliance

- Do have a BATNA – If you feel like you are constantly fighting fires and always have minimum time to prepare take some downtime right now. Consider the markets you are generally negotiating in and list alternative suppliers and/or customers that buy or sell similar services/products. Keep this list close to you in your negotiation file for easy access.

- Do contact Sue@sueprestontraining.com – I will send you a quick and dirty method of preparing. This can be done on the back of a note pad within 10 minutes and still provide structure and focus to your Negotiation.

- Do have a generic Take and Give list – In your next team meeting organise a think tank and create a generic 'Take and Give' list. Record all the variables that could be used in your market to secure movement in your Negotiation. Not all variables will be relevant in every case but when the phone rings and you are in reactionary mode you can STOP! Open your negotiation file and at a glance have some ideas on leverage tools.

The little book of Negotiation Brilliance

DON'TS

- **Don't invite the other party to put their marker down first** – This is a competitive market where you know your ground. You are familiar with any price fluctuations and you are knowledgeable about the product and/or service. You do not have time to waste on the other party putting a high marker down for you to slowly chip away at until you reach somewhere near your target.

- **Don't rush the meeting** – Take control and manage the pace of the Negotiation. Use tactics such as break-off even if just to buy yourself a couple of minutes to think. Remember summarising as you go along to keep yourself and the deal on track

- **Don't use connectors** – If you say I'm looking for a reduction in price of between 4 and 5%. The Seller will ignore your 5% request and focus only on the possibility of 4%. Another example would be if you are a seller and you pitch your widget at a price point of somewhere between £2.50 and £3.50 per unit, the buyer will ignore your £3.50 and focus only on £2.50.

The little book of Negotiation Brilliance

- **Don't get greedy** – Know when to stop. If you have hit your aims and objectives. Agree and move on. If you push too hard the other party might walk away and your time has been lost and you have to start all over again.

An Emergency preparation kit for time starved negotiators

1. Only accept 'reactionary' negotiations if they sit in a leverage, competitive market.
2. Have some generic templates and hold them in a negotiation file for easy access.
3. Contact Sue@sueprestontraining.com for a quick and straightforward template for those who are fighting fires.
4. Put your marker down and invite a response then sit back and listen. It's a competitive market and they want the business so if they can deliver to your requirements they will.
5. Cross check the targets you have set and ensure they are challenging but sensible. If you start too far out of the bargaining arena you will soak up a great deal of time with unnecessary leaps and bounds to get a deal.

The little book of Negotiation Brilliance

6. If you walk away make sure you thank the other party as you don't know when you might need them in the future.
7. Do your research and leg work in quieter times, use your team and colleagues for ideas.
8. Consider your personal impact and presence. Care not to come across as rushed or unprepared.

The little book of Negotiation Brilliance

(APPENDIX 3)

'ONE PAGE' TEAM DOCUMENT

Negotiation: Date:
Team Members:

➡ Overall Aim/objective of the Negotiation

➡ Key conditioning statement to manage the other party expectations

➡ Green light Information 'Gives'

➡ Red light Information 'Nevers'

The little book of Negotiation Brilliance

(APPENDIX 4)
NEGOTIATION REVIEW PHASE

Supplier: Projected Savings:

Actual Savings: Value Add achieved:

What went well?	
What didn't go well?	
What would I do differently next time?	
How did we measure up against our Utopia – Likely – No-Go plan?	

The little book of Negotiation Brilliance

NEGOTIATION APPLIED

Just for fun complete the following applied learning exercises. These are real life scenarios that need unravelling. Read the scenario and choose the option you would consider to be the correct course of action in such a situation. Once completed feel free to contact me at Sue@sueprestontraining.com with any questions or to compare your answers with mine. Enjoy!

MID NEGOTIATION
You are mid Negotiation and have presented your compelling argument to support your position. The other party seemed to listen intently but now silence has fallen. Which of the following would you do?
1. Repeat your argument to ensure they are convinced
2. Pose a question to the other party to check their understanding
3. Maintain the silence
4. Call a break for the other party to think
5. Express your desire for an agreement

The little book of Negotiation Brilliance

CAR SALES

You are buying a new car. You have been with the salesperson for 2 hours and have built a great rapport. After the test drive you arrive back at the showroom to be given the same price as when you left. You place your utopia position on the table and the salesperson goes off to talk to the manager. The Manager then appears saying "We are not able to get to your target" How might you respond?

1. Well, that's my budget and I can't move
2. This is my final offer. If you don't accept it, I will go to another garage
3. Show empathy to his position and then repeat your position
4. Ask "Under what circumstances could you get to my target"?
5. Walk out and say nothing

The little book of Negotiation Brilliance

CHIT CHAT

You have a Negotiation scheduled and meet the other party at reception. On the way to the meeting room, should you?
1. Tell them what you are looking for today
2. Keep discussion to small talk, journey, weather etc
3. Maintain a friendly approach whilst managing their expectations regarding your organisation's challenging targets
4. Leave them waiting in the coffee area

PAY RISE
It's the day of your performance review and you are aware of others in your team being paid more than you. This is your chance to secure a pay rise. Do you say?
- I know it's a big ask but is it ok if I request a pay rise?
- I have prepared my proposed revenue generation to the business for the next 12 months and a pay increase would only cost 2% of the total revenue
- I work in an unfair environment where my peers are earning more than me. I demand a pay rise
- Threaten to leave unless you have a pay rise with immediate effect

The little book of Negotiation Brilliance

AND FINALLY, at the start of the book you answered a series of generic negotiation questions from your current knowledge. This time answer the same questions again using strategies, techniques and tactics you have read in this book, compare any differences and create an action plan of changes you need to make to your negotiation approach. If there are any outstanding questions that you are still unable to answer or any bespoke questions within your 'REAL' environment send them through and I will respond with detailed answers and offer a 'free' 30 minute virtual coaching session. (sue@sueprestontraining.com).

- When's the right time to put your stake in the ground?
- How should I negotiate with a monopoly supplier?
- How do you get a buyer to say 'YES'?
- How do you regain control?
- What should you do when you hit stalemate?
- How do you know the other party's 'true' range of objectives?
- What are the key signals of movement?
- Is there ever a time where you just put all your cards on the table, refuse to play the game and just tell the other party what you need?
- Where is the best location for a Negotiation? Home or Away?
- What is the optimum number for a successful negotiation team?

The little book of Negotiation Brilliance

- What are the responsibilities and key roles in team negotiations?
- Why are some people innately good negotiators?
- How do I secure a better deal when I need the product/service delivered quickly?
- How does supply and demand affect the outcome of Negotiation?
- What is a good amount of time to set aside for Preparation and Planning?
- What is the difference between internal and external negotiations?
- How does culture affect negotiations?
- How do you deal with difficult people during a negotiation?

I hope you enjoyed this book and that it has added value to your future negotiation strategies. This little book certainly packs a punch and is designed to supply you with an awesome toolkit for your next Negotiation.

I would like to thank all of my mentors who I have learned so much from over the years. I would also like to thank a 'partner in crime' who I used to work with most days. He knows who he is, we used to travel the world teaching people on how to raise the bar on their commercial negotiation capability. He is a great friend, an awesome guy and the best mentor. Without our journey this book wouldn't have been possible.

The little book of Negotiation Brilliance

Stay in touch and let me know how these techniques work for you in your real world.

This was Sue Preston (Sue@sueprestontraining.com)

THANK YOU and Happy Negotiating!

Printed in Great Britain
by Amazon